OIL

Will It Last?

JIM PIPE

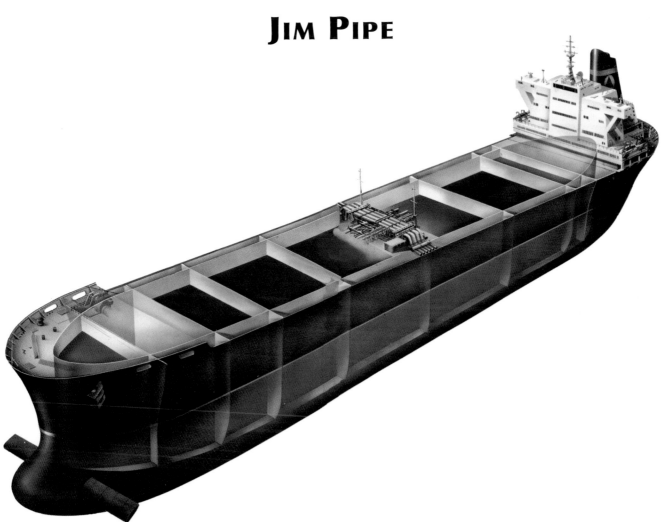

ALADDIN/WATTS
LONDON • SYDNEY

Contents

© Aladdin Books Ltd 2010

Designed and produced by
Aladdin Books Ltd
PO Box 53987
London SW15 2SF

First published in 2010
by Franklin Watts
338 Euston Road
London NW1 3BH

Franklin Watts Australia
Level 17/207 Kent Street
Sydney NSW 2000

Franklin Watts is a division of
Hachette Children's Books,
an Hachette UK company.
www.hachette.co.uk

All rights reserved
Printed in Malaysia

Scientific consultant: Rob Bowden

A catalogue record for
this book is available
from the British Library.

Dewey Classification:
333.9'232

ISBN 978 07496 9079 3

What's the Issue?

Oil is the world's most important source of liquid fuel, and, along with other fossils fuels such as coal and gas, provides most of our energy. However, burning these fossil fuels releases gases that add to global warming, as well as polluting the air. It is also getting harder, and more expensive, to get oil out of the ground.

Meanwhile, the world is using more and more energy. The challenge we face now is to find cheap, reliable alternatives to oil and other fossil fuels without adding to our environmental problems. Renewable energy sources such as wind and solar power are part of the solution, but so is learning to use fossil fuels such as oil more efficiently and with lower emissions levels.

◑ **Oil** *provides energy for most of the world's transport.*

Oil Production Platforms

Why Oil?

Oil field

Oil is one of the world's most important resources. Most of the things you see around you depend on oil, from cars, planes and computers to food and home heating. The problem is, for the last 25 years the world has been using oil much faster than it is finding new sources.

Though oil won't run out, it will become much harder to get out of the ground. Most experts predict that the amount of oil the world produces will peak in the next ten years. To avoid an energy crisis, the world needs to find new energy sources.

⚐ Finding Oil

Finding new oil fields isn't easy. There are few obvious clues on the surface. Oil can lie hidden below deserts, jungles, swamps or polar ice.

Fossil Fuels Warm Earth

In the short term, some countries are planning to replace oil with other fossil fuels such as gas and coal. However, burning fossil fuels adds to global warming – the carbon dioxide it releases acts like a giant window, trapping the Sun's heat and pushing up temperatures.

Most scientists predict that global warming will have very damaging effects, such as rising sea levels caused by melting ice, and flooding, droughts, crop failures and an increase in storms.

Pumpjack

OIL ENERGY: For

- An oil-fuelled power station can be built almost anywhere, so long as you can get large amounts of oil to it.
- Large amounts of electricity can be generated in a single oil-fired power station, compared to the large area needed for a wind or solar farm.
- Large tankers and pipelines can transport oil to power stations easily.
- In most countries, the refineries and petrol stations needed to use oil are already built.

OIL ENERGY: Against

- Burning oil releases carbon dioxide, adding to the "greenhouse effect" that warms the Earth.
- Oil is not renewable. Once it's gone, it's gone. The amount of oil the world uses has nearly doubled every 20 years since 1900.
- As oil gets harder to find and take out of the ground, it will get more expensive.
- Oil isn't just a fuel – it's also needed to make fertilisers, plastics and many other products.
- Many poor countries can't afford to build their own pipelines, refineries or petrol stations.

▷ Black Gold

Oil has been called "black gold" as it is so valuable. As the reserves of oil run out, oil prices will rise. Everything from travel, heating, agriculture, trade and anything made of plastic will get more expensive.

While we rely so much on oil for transport fuel, any product that needs to be moved long distances, such as food, will also cost more.

◁ Nodding Donkey

A pumpjack is used to pump oil from below the ground. It is also known as a "nodding donkey" because it moves slowly up and down as it pumps the oil.

ENERGY FACTS:
How Much Oil?

- Oil is measured in barrels. One barrel of oil = **159** litres (about 80 large water bottles or enough to fill up the petrol tanks of about 4 family cars).
- In 2008, there were an estimated **1,258,000** million (1,258 billion) barrels of oil still under the ground in known reserves.
- The world uses around **84.5** million barrels of oil each day.
- Some countries use a lot more oil than others. The United States has 5 per cent of the world's population but uses 21 per cent of its energy, including **19.4** million barrels of oil each day.

What Is Oil?

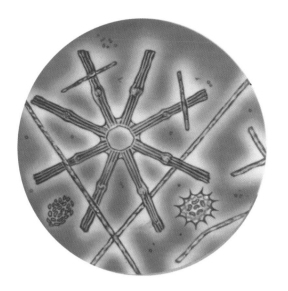

🜂 Plankton

Microscopic plankton living in seas today are similar to prehistoric plankton from which oil comes. Though tiny, plankton can appear in such large numbers they can be seen from space as a blue swirl.

Crude oil, also called petroleum, or petrol (meaning "rock oil" in Latin), is the rocky remains of tiny sea creatures and plants called plankton, that floated in the oceans millions of years ago.

When these microscopic organisms died, their bodies sank to the ocean floor. Over many millions of years, the rotting remains turned into fossils that were crushed and cooked underground, turning them into oil. This crude oil has been found deep underground in many parts of the world, though the colour and thickness of the oil differs from place to place.

How Oil Forms

1 Millions of years ago much of the Earth was sea, and as plants and animals in the seas die, they sink to the sea floor and rot.

2 Gradually, mud and sand pile up on top of the rotting remains. The weight and pressure turn the remains into crude oil, and squeeze it upwards and outwards.

3 The rising oil seeps upwards through spongy rock such as sandstone and limestone.

When the oil reaches hard rock that stops it from flowing, it is trapped underground in a pool or reservoir. Salt domes also act as natural traps as they do not let oil flow past.

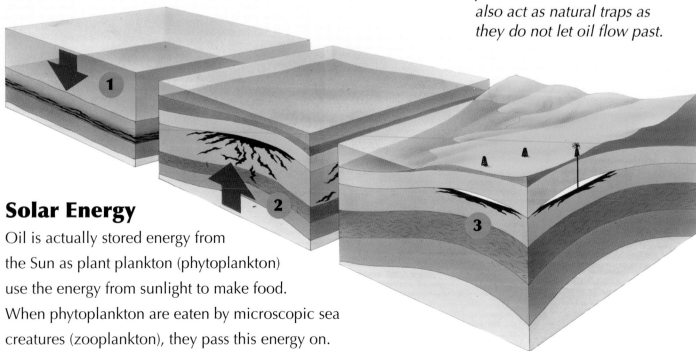

Solar Energy

Oil is actually stored energy from the Sun as plant plankton (phytoplankton) use the energy from sunlight to make food. When phytoplankton are eaten by microscopic sea creatures (zooplankton), they pass this energy on.

Underground Pressure

In some places, underground pressure forces oil to seep to the surface. Here it forms lakes of bitumen, known as pitch lakes.

Most oil gets trapped by a layer of hard rock. It collects underground in a huge reservoir, like a can of fizzy drink shaken but not opened. When you drill down through the hard rock to the reservoir, the underground pressure makes the oil gush through the hole made by the drill. The liquid that rises up to the platform is a mix of crude oil, natural gas, water and sediments.

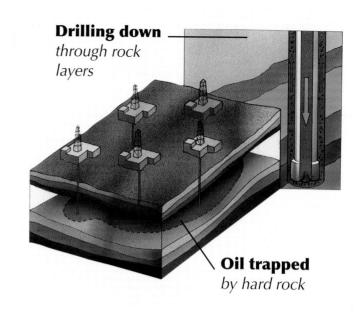

Drilling down *through rock layers*

Oil trapped *by hard rock*

◖◗ Tar Sands

Oil is found on every continent and in the seabeds of the world's oceans, but it's getting harder to find. People are looking for other sources of oil, such as the tar sands of Canada (left). These are natural mixtures of sand or clay, water and bitumen.

Another source of oil is a rock known as oil shale, found in Estonia, China and Brazil. When heated to high temperatures, the shale turns into a synthetic oil that can be burnt in power stations.

ENERGY FACTS: Crude Oil

When oil comes straight from the ground, we call it crude oil. It is usually black or dark brown, but green, red or brown oils are not uncommon. "Heavy" oils are thick and sticky, while "light" oils are thin and light enough to float on water. Crude oil is actually a mix of:
• Liquids such as kerosene and gasoline
• Sticky materials such as bitumen (pitch)
• Gases, such as propane, butane and methane. These appear in crude oil as billions of tiny bubbles, making the oil even more liquid.

Bitumen is the black, treacly tar used to cover roads.

Drilling for Oil

Geologists (earth scientists) find oil in many different ways, using satellite images and readings taken on the ground or at sea. They also set off explosives to find where pockets of oil might be trapped between layers of rock.

Once oil is found, test wells are drilled to trace the size and shape of the field. Samples of oil are tested to see its quality and how it will flow. There is no guarantee of finding oil – the chances of a successful strike are just one in ten.

The Search for Oil

1 Aerial/Satellite Photographs
Geologists can tell a lot about underground rocks from satellite and aerial photos, and from the lie of the land.

2 Shock Waves
Small explosions reveal the pattern of rocks as the shock waves they produce bounce back to the surface. The vibrations are charted on a computer or graph and point out where pockets of oil might be trapped between layers of rock.

3 Test Well
A sample of rock called a core is brought up to the surface and checked for oil. If there are tiny drops of oil clinging to the rock a test well is drilled. In the early 19th century, "wildcat" wells were drilled in random sites in the hope of striking oil.

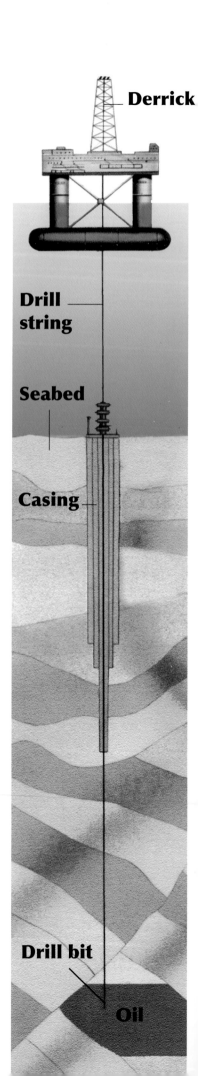

Derrick

Drill string

Seabed

Casing

Drill bit

Oil

▼ Drilling Rigs

Drilling rigs are used to drill into the ground to reach oil. A steel frame, known as a derrick, is built to hold the drilling equipment. The drilling is done by a sharp-toothed bit. This spins up to 250 times a minute, cutting into the rock. As it digs into the ground, linked steel pipes are added, called a drill string. Mud is pumped down the pipes. This keeps the bit cool and brings broken rock to the surface.

◖ Offshore Rigs

Drilling an oil well offshore requires rigs on floating tanks or special ships. These rigs only look for oil, they do not pump it. Some are huge and can drill through thousands of metres of the Earth's crust. Hoists in the rig can lift thousands of tonnes of pipe. Other equipment can force acid, sand or carbon dioxide into reservoirs to help extract the oil.

◗ Production Platform

Once a rig has struck oil, a platform is built to produce the oil. Platforms with giant steel legs are used in waters less than 400 m deep.
In very deep waters, floating platforms use huge buoyancy tanks to stay afloat.

1 Helicopter pad
2 Derrick
3 Flare (burns off unwanted gas)
4 Living quarters
5 Drill string
6 Steel legs
7 Pipes
8 Seabed

Transporting Oil

When a drill has almost reached the pocket of oil, tubing is lowered into the well. A small explosion blasts away the rock above the pocket. Oil gushes up the tubing and is channelled to a storage tank. Gas found at the same time is separated from the oil as it comes to the surface.

However, oil is often found in remote places such as in the middle of deserts, seas or frozen lands. It must be transported by tankers or pipelines from the oil well to the refinery. Here it is separated into different oils and gases. The refined products then go to customers by pipeline or by road in smaller tankers.

◑ At the Pump

The oil we put into our cars has travelled a long way from where it was drilled.

◐ Pipelines

Oil is transported around the world by giant pipelines that run along the seabed or across land. The Trans-Alaska pipeline runs 1,300 km across Alaska, crossing three mountain ranges and 800 rivers and streams. Pumping stations along the pipeline keep the oil flowing regularly.

Oil tanker

◑ Super Tankers

The biggest ships, known as ultra large crude carriers (ULCCs), can carry up to 3.4 million barrels of oil in one voyage (the same as 16,000 truckloads). However, they need very large ports to dock in, as they can take 8 km to stop.

Safety Measures

To cut down the risk of oil spills, modern tankers are double-hulled, with an extra space between the hull and the storage tanks. To avoid fires, as a tank is pumped out it is filled with inert gas until the next cargo is loaded.

Double skin

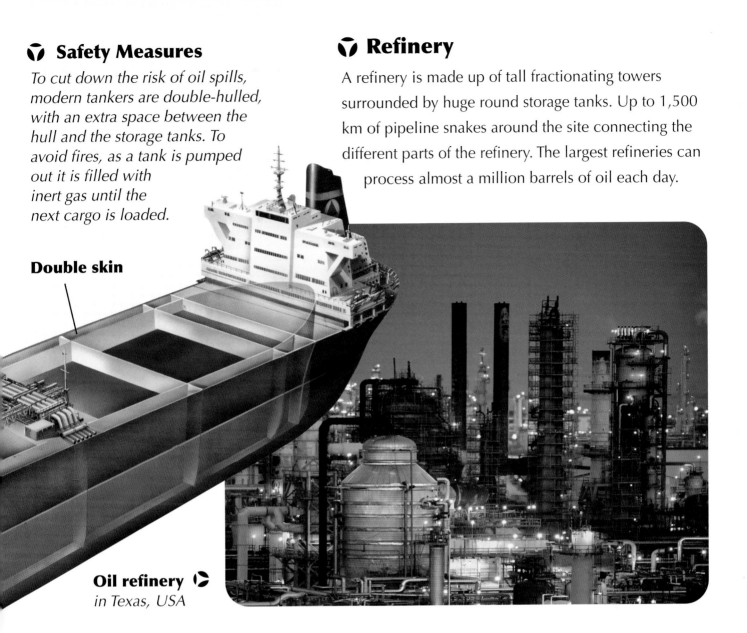

Oil refinery
in Texas, USA

Refinery

A refinery is made up of tall fractionating towers surrounded by huge round storage tanks. Up to 1,500 km of pipeline snakes around the site connecting the different parts of the refinery. The largest refineries can process almost a million barrels of oil each day.

Refining Oil

A refinery separates crude oil into different types of oil and gas, known as fractions. First the crude oil is heated to 400 °C in a furnace so it turns to gases. These pass into a tall tower called a fractionating column.

As the gases rise, they cool and turn back into liquid (condense). The tower gets cooler at the top, so different fractions turn back into liquid at different levels and collect in distilling trays. Fractions such as propane remain as gases and exit at the top of the tower.

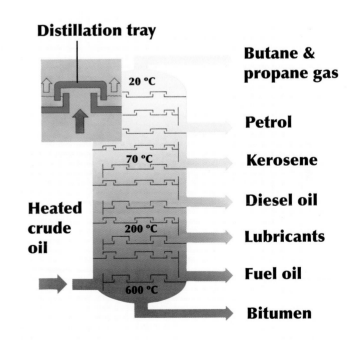

Distillation tray

Butane & propane gas

20 °C

Petrol

Kerosene

70 °C

Diesel oil

Heated crude oil

Lubricants

200 °C

Fuel oil

600 °C

Bitumen

11

Oil as a Fuel

We live in a world dominated by energy – we use it to transport us, heat and feed us, run our computers and electric machines, and build our world. Everything we buy, from plastic chairs and drugs to cars and computers, needs energy.

At the moment, oil is the source of almost 40 per cent of our energy. Oil burns easily and is easy to store. It is our main fuel for transport and for the last century has been a cheap source of energy. It is burnt in power stations to generate electricity as well as being used to heat homes, schools and workplaces.

▷ Getting Around

For the last 100 years we have depended on oil and the internal-combustion engine. Today, some 750 million cars, trucks and other vehicles roam the planet, and 90 per cent of them use oil, as it is the cheapest way to move around.

Yet much of the energy created by car engines is wasted as useless heat, noise and friction, or as unburned fumes in the exhaust.

Oil-fired Power Stations

Oil fuels 7 per cent of the world's electricity, and 20 per cent of the world's oil is burnt in power stations. When the oil is burnt it releases its energy as heat. This is used to boil water to steam. The steam is then blasted against giant turbine blades. As these turn, they drive generators, which produce electricity. However, even the most efficient power stations can only turn 40 per cent of oil's energy into electricity. Oil is also used as a fuel in factories – in some countries the blast furnaces in steel mills are fired by oil.

▽ Transport

Over 75 per cent of refined oil is made into fuels, for cars, trucks, ships and aircraft.

Big cities
gobble up oil and energy.

◆ Energy for Cities

Look at this NASA image of San Francisco, USA, from space and imagine how much energy is used to build and run a modern city. Making just one tonne of cement requires the energy from 170 litres (over a barrel) of oil.

Oil Products

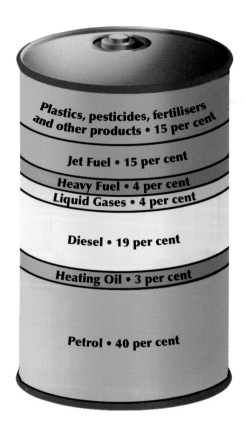

Plastics, pesticides, fertilisers and other products • 15 per cent

Jet Fuel • 15 per cent

Heavy Fuel • 4 per cent

Liquid Gases • 4 per cent

Diesel • 19 per cent

Heating Oil • 3 per cent

Petrol • 40 per cent

⚠ **Products made from a barrel of crude oil**

Oil isn't just the world's main source of energy – vast amounts of oil are used as raw materials in the manufacture of a huge range of products, from the bitumen used to cover roads, to fertilisers and pesticides. Oil is also used to make plastics, cosmetics, detergents and synthetic fibres such as polyester and nylon.

▽ On the Farm

Oil helps to feed the world. Modern agriculture depends on oil, and not just to build and run farm machines such as tractors. Oil is also used to make petrochemicals such as fertilisers and pesticides, used by farmers to help their crops grow and protect them from pests. It is also used in some animal feeds.

Spraying pesticides

ENERGY FACTS:
Oil-based Products

We take oil for granted. Imagine a world without these products:

• Plastic objects – toothbrushes, shoes, CDs, computers, toys, tubs, blinds, sunglasses, toilet seats, bubble wrap, telephones, tents, hoses, luggage and most food packaging
• Vinyl – LP records and wallpaper
• Clothes made from synthetic fabrics such as nylon, polyester and Lycra (spandex)

• Detergents – washing powder, washing-up liquid
• Sun creams, lipsticks, face creams, soaps, perfumes, mascara, hair sprays, shampoos and even false eyelashes all contain by-products of oil.
• Synthetic carpets and flooring
• Motorbike helmets
• Disposable nappies
• Bubble-gum
• Balloons
• Tyres
• Crayons
• Ink
• Parachutes

Plastics

Most plastics are made from oil. Petroleum is transported from the oil refinery to chemical factories that turn it into synthetic resins. The resins are then heated, pressed and squirted into moulds to make the finished products (right), from the flexible plastics used in bags and wrappings to the hard plastics used in toys, computers and suitcases.

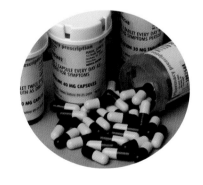

Healthcare

Crude oil is an important ingredient in many medicines, such as pain relievers. Oil-based plastics are used to make heart valves and glasses.

Renewable Alternatives

In the past, crops such as sugar cane (left) were used as fertilisers. These are renewable as they can be grown again. Scientists are also developing replacements for other oil-based products. Lignin, found in wood, can be mixed with hemp or wood fibres and wax to create a strong, non-toxic substitute for plastic.

Oil Pollution

Smog over Los Angeles, California, USA

Oil pollutes the air when it is burned, releasing the greenhouse gas carbon dioxide that adds to global warming. Oil-fired power stations and vehicles also release sulphur and nitrogen gases. These drift high into the air and dissolve into water droplets, creating the acid rain that damages rivers and forests.

Oil spilt into rivers or oceans can harm wildlife, and exploring and drilling for oil may disturb land and ocean habitats. However, new drilling techniques allow a single well to produce oil from much bigger areas, while new technologies have greatly reduced the number and size of areas disturbed by drilling.

◑ Smog

Cars and trucks that run on petrol or diesel release fumes and gases such as sulphur dioxide. Diesel also gives out tiny particles such as soot. These can form a smog over large cities, especially in cities such as Los Angeles (above) that are surrounded by hills. In London in 1952, more than 4,000 people died in polluted smog, known as "pea soup".

◑ A Danger to Wildlife

Hundreds of millions of litres of oil end up in the seas every year, whether poured down the drain or from cleaning ships' holds. Oil spills from tankers are very damaging as the oil forms a thick black slick that kills large numbers of birds and other sea animals.

In 2002, the oil tanker the *Prestige* sank off Spain's coast creating a huge oil spill. Another 77,000 tonnes of oil sank with the ship to the bottom. Thousands of seabirds died as 900 km of shoreline were affected.

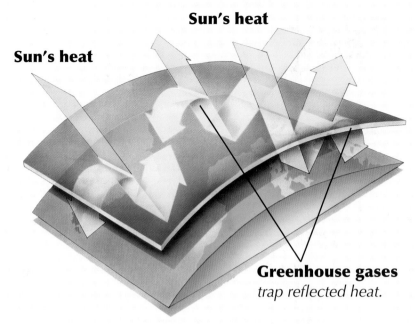

Sun's heat

Sun's heat

Greenhouse gases trap reflected heat.

◀ Greenhouse Gases

When the Sun's energy reaches the Earth, some is reflected back to space, but most reaches the Earth's surface. Once absorbed, this energy is sent back into the atmosphere.

Here greenhouse gases such as carbon dioxide and methane trap this heat in the same way that glass traps heat in a greenhouse, causing our world to heat up. As burning fossil fuels such as oil creates large amounts of carbon dioxide (CO_2), it is adding to global warming.

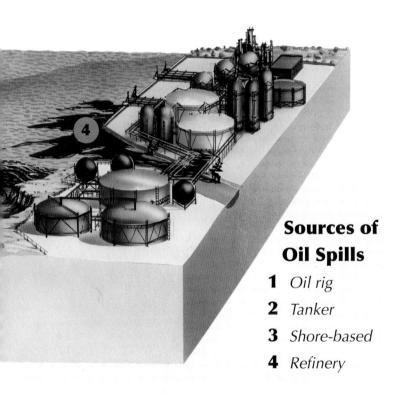

◀ Refineries

Refineries can also cause problems as strict controls are needed to prevent dangerous waste gases such as sulphur dioxide escaping. Care must also be taken so that the waste from refineries does not pollute seas, rivers and lakes.

Sources of Oil Spills

1 *Oil rig*
2 *Tanker*
3 *Shore-based*
4 *Refinery*

Adding to Global Warming

Scientists estimate that global temperatures in the last 100 years have already risen by 1 °C. This may not sound like much, but if they rise another 2 °C it will cause widespread forest fires, prairies will turn to dustbowls and tropical diseases such as malaria will spread. Global warming will also lead to spreading deserts and drought. Rising sea levels will force people away from low-lying coastal areas.

> **ENERGY FACTS:**
> **How Can We Stop Global Warming?**
>
> • Even if we stopped pumping carbon dioxide (CO_2) into the atmosphere today, it would take 200 years for nature to reduce the CO_2 back to levels that existed before the Industrial Revolution.
>
> • The amount of CO_2 being released is rising. Today, we are producing 6.3 billion tonnes of CO_2 a year. This amount is expected to increase to 12 billion tonnes by 2030.
>
> • The United States, China and the EU account for over half of the world's CO_2 emissions.
>
> • Oil-rich states such as Qatar, Kuwait and the United Arab Emirates release the most CO_2 emissions per person.

How Much Is Left?

Oil experts predict that the world's known oil reserves will last for 60 years at most. Oil is getting harder to find – people have been drilling holes since the 1900s and new reservoirs the size of the giant Ghawar oil field in Saudi Arabia are unlikely to be discovered. Oil companies are already being forced into tough terrain deep below the sea, into the Arctic wilderness and in the jungles of Borneo.

Oil won't run out tomorrow, but things will get harder as prices rise and the world's economy needs a steady supply of energy to keep it running. Something needs to be done before the world reaches "peak oil" (see page 19) – whether it's in 5 years' or 25 years' time.

◭ Icy climate

This oil well is in northern Alaska where temperatures can drop to -60 °C in winter.

Jack 2 Oil Field

◖ Digging Deeper

One of the biggest finds in recent years is in the Gulf of Mexico. A test well named "Jack 2" discovered oil 430 km off the coast and 10,000 metres below the ocean surface, a sign that easier sources have already been exhausted. This field may hold up to 15 billion barrels of oil (less than a year's supply for the world).

Tar Sands in Alberta, Canada

Better Techniques

Oil companies are getting better at finding and extracting oil:

1 *New production methods can refine "heavy oil" from Venezuela and Canadian tar sands.*
2 *Drilling can be done in almost any climate – on the frozen Arctic tundra or from a floating platform 10 km or more above the seabed.*
3 *Oil firms can now can get much more from a given field – up to 80 per cent compared with just 30 per cent in the 1970s.*
4 *Satellites, global positioning systems, remote sensing devices and 3-D and 4-D seismic technologies make it possible to discover oil while drilling fewer wells.*

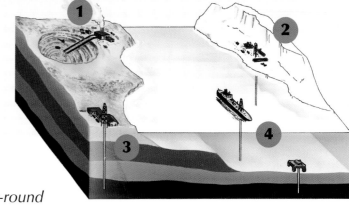

Drilling Under the Ice

Over half of the Arctic Ocean was covered in year-round ice in the mid-1980s. Today, the ice cap is much smaller. Energy companies are hoping to profit from the melting ice as it will become much easier to search for oil.

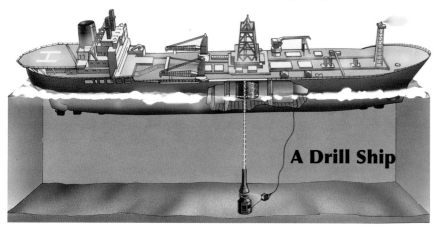

A Drill Ship

Arctic Oil

The Arctic region may hold large amounts of oil, but drilling and extracting it in deep ice-covered waters, thousands of kilometres from a tanker port, will create big challenges. A massive pipeline might need to be built, adding to the cost of finding the oil.

Too Expensive?

Enormous reserves of oil have been found in the tar sands of Alberta, Canada, but this oil is much more expensive to take out of the ground and refine.

It also uses about 20 times as much energy as it takes to extract oil from a conventional well. So it's only worth producing this oil when oil prices are very high.

ENERGY FACTS: What Is Peak Oil?

Peak oil describes the point at which the amount of oil being produced starts to go down. It has taken perhaps 100 years to reach this point, but as we are using oil faster and faster, we may use the rest up in the next 40-60 years.

The Future of Oil?

Energy has been so cheap over the last 30 years that many people in the United States and Europe have bigger houses, larger, more powerful cars and more electrical appliances – increasing their energy use all the time. People in less developed nations all want these things too. By 2032, the amount of energy the world will be using is expected to double.

As the demand for oil rises from less developed countries such as China, India and Brazil, where will the energy supply come from? Many governments around the world are now encouraging renewable energy sources such as wind power and biofuels. Others are turning to nuclear power.

▷ Oil Guzzlers

Machines have become a lot more energy-efficient in the last 50 years. However, there are many more cars on the road today and in the 2000s they got a lot bigger. SUVs consume large amounts of oil. People are also driving more, on average about 20,000 kilometres a year, partly because more are commuting to work.

SUV *(Sports Utility Vehicle)*

⬩ Caspian Sea Oil Field
A pipeline opened in 2005 connects oil fields near the Caspian Sea with the Mediterranean Sea. It runs for over 1,760 km and carries a million barrels a day.

Energy Security

Many countries can't produce their own oil, or not enough to meet their needs, so they rely on oil-producing countries for their supplies. These countries can make the price of oil rise just by taking less oil out of the ground. Future oil supplies could also be threatened by natural disasters or terrorist attacks. Many governments are now investing in local supplies of energy, such as biofuels and wind power.

Getting the Balance Right

The problem for governments today is finding the right balance among the three Es: energy, environment and economy. They need energy for their economy to grow, but they also need to use it as efficiently as possible to protect the environment.

Fighting Over Oil

The race for oil is already getting more competitive. The US invasion of Iraq secured supplies of oil in the region for the West, and Russia and Iran have been in a diplomatic war to control oil coming from Central Asian countries such as Kazakhstan and Azerbaijan.

There will be no winners; oil is running out and the new sources are nothing like the giant reserves previously found in the Middle East.

Coal-fired power station

Using Less Oil

⚠ Cleaner Coal?

Carbon capture is a process that stores the greenhouse gas carbon dioxide (CO_2) created by burning coal. The CO_2 is removed using chemicals and turned into a liquid, ready for storage underground. However, getting carbon capture to work on a large scale may be difficult.

The energy crisis probably won't be solved by one amazing new piece of technology but by a combination of using renewable sources and conserving energy. In the short term, replacing oil with coal will only add to global warming. However, natural gas is still plentiful, is 33 per cent cleaner than oil and can be turned into a liquid fuel for cars.

We also need to learn how to get the most out of the energy we use. Many governments around the world are now trying to encourage people to use less energy, by providing grants to make homes more energy-efficient and introducing a "carbon tax" that taxes firms for the amount of fossil fuels they burn.

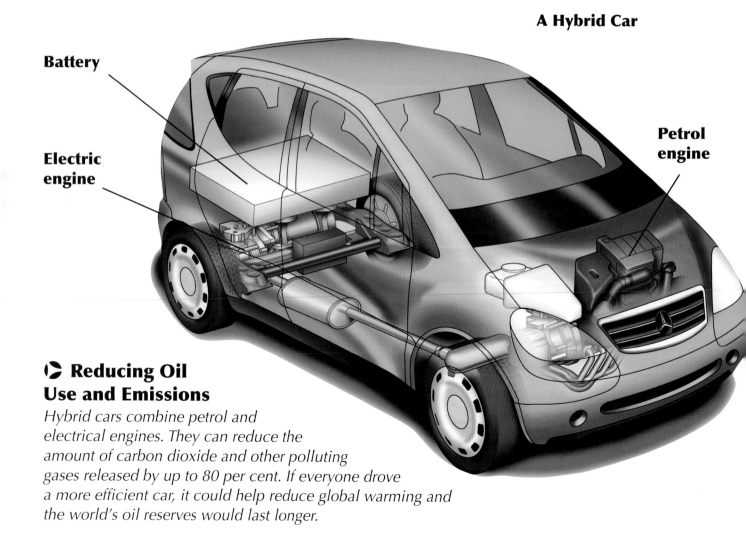

A Hybrid Car

Battery

Electric engine

Petrol engine

▷ Reducing Oil Use and Emissions

Hybrid cars combine petrol and electrical engines. They can reduce the amount of carbon dioxide and other polluting gases released by up to 80 per cent. If everyone drove a more efficient car, it could help reduce global warming and the world's oil reserves would last longer.

Being Energy Efficient

Today's appliances use half the energy they did in the 1970s. By the end of the 21st century, 30 per cent of new energy could come from such savings.

Simple changes, such as energy-efficient light bulbs, can make a big difference. If everyone in the UK bought the most efficient washing machines and other household goods, it would be the same as taking 1.4 million cars off the road.

Working Together

We've learned to save energy before. After the oil crisis in the 1970s, air conditioners were adapted to use less power but with the same cooling effect, and new building codes led to double-glazing, better insulation and more effective heating systems. So even though the US economy boomed in the early 1980s, oil demand fell by one sixth. But when oil became cheap again in the mid-1980s, people stopped conserving energy.

A Home of the Future?

1 *Wind power (microturbine)*
2 *Solar panels*
3 *Recycling plastics*
4 *Using biogas from waste*
5 *Water power*
6 *Insulating walls, roofs and floors, and energy efficient lighting (not shown)*
7 *Double-glazed windows*
8 *Electric or hybrid cars*
9 *Efficient heating system*

ENERGY FACTS: Who Uses What?

This list shows how much oil an average person consumed in these countries in 2006. People in more developed countries tend to use a lot more energy.

Saudi Arabia: 28.9 barrels per year
United States: 24 barrels per year
Japan: 14.8 barrels per year
Germany: 12 barrels per year
UK: 10.9 barrels per year
Brazil: 4.3 barrels per year
China: 1.9 barrels per year
India: 0.8 barrels per year

Reuse, Recycle, Renew

The huge amount of rubbish the modern world discards is also a terrible waste of energy. Recycling saves a lot of the energy used to extract raw materials such as aluminium from the ground.

The plastic bag levy in European countries such as Ireland led to a huge reduction in plastic bags (all made from oil) as people began using reusable cloth bags or biodegradable paper bags instead.

Life After Oil

In the long term, oil, gas and coal will all run out or become too expensive to get out of the ground. Wind farms, however, are an increasingly cheap way to produce clean, renewable electricity. By 2030, wind and solar power could provide 20 per cent of the world's energy, ten times the amount today. Biofuels, fuels made from plants or algae, may provide the liquid fuels needed in cars and planes. All this new technology will cost money. It will be cheaper – and better for the planet – if we also learn to use less energy.

Fuel Cells

Cars need liquid fuel and one alternative is using hydrogen in fuel cells. Unlike batteries, fuel cells don't store electrical energy. Instead, they turn energy from chemical reactions between oxygen and hydrogen into electrical energy.

Hydrogen can be produced by wind turbines and biofuels. But it's costly to produce and hard to handle. It must be compressed under very high pressure or refrigerated to a supercooled liquid.

Slowing Global Warming

If we can find a cheap and efficient way to produce energy without fossil fuels it will help to reduce air and water pollution and smog-related illnesses. It will also reduce the damage caused by global warming, such as floods and droughts.

Flooding
Due to the heavy rainfalls, the town of Bansko in Bulgaria was flooded by a nearby river.

Biofuels

Some people think biofuels – fuels made from plants and animal waste – may solve the oil crisis. However, growing a lot more energy crops such as sugar cane (right) would use up valuable farmland.

Scientists are now working on a new generation of biofuels made from algae (green pond scum) that can be grown on land unsuitable for agriculture. Algae also soaks up carbon dioxide so these new biofuels could combat global warming.

Harvesting sugar cane

The Nuclear Option

Nuclear power provides 18 per cent of the world's electricity. Though it does not produce CO_2, it's hard to find a site as few people want a nuclear power station nearby. Nuclear plants are also expensive to build though relatively cheap to run. There are also problems with where to put spent nuclear waste, the danger from terrorists and dwindling supplies of uranium, the fuel used in nuclear power stations.

Wind Power

Wind power is already big business. Wind farms can be built on any scale, from rooftop turbines to giant wind farms with hundreds of big turbines. But it takes thousands of wind turbines to replace an oil-fired power station.

Wind Turbines

Solar power

Solar power could one day solve all of our energy needs, but today it costs five times as much as coal-fired power. One possible solution is a film covering windows and sides of buildings that converts sunlight to electricity.

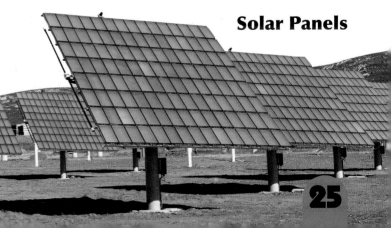

Solar Panels

HOT OFF THE PRESS!

Undersea robots

■ Oil companies are depending more and more on hi-tech robots as the search for oil takes them into dangerous Arctic and deep-sea waters. Undersea robots are used for many different tasks, from inspecting pipelines and other structures to collecting soil samples up to 150 metres below the sea floor. Some robots are designed for heavy lifting jobs while others have a range of different tools onboard, so there is no need to return to the surface between jobs.

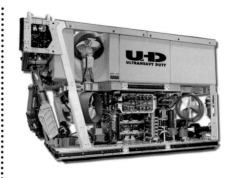

An ROV (remotely operated underwater vehicle) designed for heavy work on the seabed

Speed without oil

■ A new electric bike weighing just 102 kg can reach speeds up to 100 km/h thanks to its small but extremely powerful battery pack. The "Zero" motorbike can be charged from an ordinary household socket in four hours. It produces less than an eighth of the CO_2 pollution per kilometre than a bike that runs on petrol.

What do you do with an old oil rig?

■ In the "rig-to-reefs" scheme, old offshore rigs are toppled and left on the sea floor. Here they become artificial reefs. Within a year, the sunken rigs are covered with barnacles, coral, sponges, clams and other sea creatures.

Oil rig eco-hotel

In a recent competition, architects came up with a scheme for turning an old oil rig into an offshore eco-hotel that is powered by wind and wave power. The guest rooms would be built on land then transported to the rig on a container ship.

Zero motorbike

Swedish ready for a world without oil

■ The Swedish government plans to stop using oil by 2020, and Sweden will eventually be run on renewable energy. This country of nine million people may become the first industrialised nation to become oil-free – and without building any new nuclear power plants.

If successful, Sweden will avoid the rise in oil prices as oil becomes harder to get out of the ground. The country already gets most of its electricity from hydro-electric and nuclear power. Almost all its heating now comes from schemes which distribute steam or hot water generated by geothermal energy or waste heat.

Sweden is not alone in trying to end its addiction to oil. Iceland hopes by 2050 to power all its cars and boats with hydrogen made from renewable electricity, while Brazil intends to power 80 per cent of its vehicles with biofuel made from sugar cane within five years.

The first oil tanker was built in Sweden in 1878. But oil tankers may be an increasingly rare sight in Sweden.

Canadian tar sands

■ The scheme to remove tar sands from Alberta, Canada is the largest industrial project in human history. It may also be the most destructive. The mining methods release at least three times as much CO_2 as regular oil wells and are causing huge areas of forest to be cut down. Current projects will see 3 million

" The tar sands scheme is the largest industrial project in human history – and possibly the most destructive. **"**

barrels of tar sands oil produced daily by 2018. For each barrel of oil up to five barrels of water are used.

Arctic oil

■ Global warming is causing the Arctic pack ice to break up and retreat, allowing ships to sail along the northern coastline of Canada for the first time. The United States, along with teams from Canada, Denmark, Greenland, Norway and Russia, can now explore the Arctic Ocean in detail. The region may hold up to 50 billion barrels of oil. That seems a lot, but it's only enough to supply the world's needs for 2 years.

US ships map the ocean floor in the Arctic Ocean.

How Oil Compares

While oil is cheap, burning it releases carbon dioxide into the atmosphere, causing pollution and global warming. Nuclear power is one alternative, but reactors are expensive and they create dangerous waste. Biofuels, along with other renewables such as wind power, are a clean source of energy, but they supply just a small part of the world's energy needs.

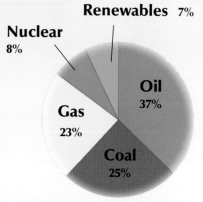

Renewables 7%
Nuclear 8%
Oil 37%
Gas 23%
Coal 25%

World Energy Sources

NON-RENEWABLE ENERGY SOURCES

Oil

For:

Oil is cheap and easy to store, transport and use.

Against:

Oil is not renewable and it is getting more expensive to get out of the ground. Burning oil releases large amounts of greenhouse gases. Oil spills, especially at sea, cause severe pollution.

Gas

For:

Gas is relatively cheap, and produces less greenhouses gases than oil and coal.

Against:

Burning gas releases carbon dioxide. Gas is not renewable and the world's natural gas reserves are limited. Gas pipelines can disrupt the migration routes of animals such as caribou.

Coal

For:

Coal is cheap and supplies of coal are expected to last another 150 years.

Against:

Coal-fired power stations give off the most greenhouse gases. They also produce sulphur dioxide, creating acid rain. Coal mining can be very destructive to the landscape.

Nuclear

For:

Nuclear power is constant and reliable, and doesn't contribute to global warming.

Against:

Not renewable as uranium (the main nuclear fuel) will eventually run out. Nuclear waste is so dangerous it must be buried for thousands of years. Also the risk of a nuclear accident.

Biofuels

For:
Biofuels are cheap and renewable and can be made from waste.

Against:
Growing biofuels from energy crops reduces the land available for food and uses up vital resources such as fresh water. Like fossil fuels, biofuels can produce greenhouse gases.

Wind Power

For:
Wind power needs no fuel, it's renewable and doesn't pollute.

Against:
Wind is unpredictable, so wind farms need a back-up power supply. Possible danger to bird flocks. It takes thousands of wind turbines to produce the same power as a nuclear plant.

Solar Power

For:
Solar power needs no fuel, it's renewable and doesn't pollute.

Against:
Solar power stations are very expensive as solar (photovoltaic) cells cost a lot compared to the amount of electricity they produce. They're unreliable unless used in a very sunny climate.

Hydroelectric Power

For:
Hydroelectric power needs no fuel, is renewable and doesn't pollute.

Against:
Hydroelectric power is very expensive to build. A large dam will flood a very large area upstream, impacting on animals and people there. A dam can affect water quality downstream.

Geothermal Power

For:
Geothermal power needs no fuel, it's renewable and doesn't pollute.

Against:
There aren't many suitable places for a geothermal power station as you need hot rocks of the right type and not too deep. It can "run out of steam". Underground poisonous gases can be a danger.

Tidal Power

For:
Tidal power needs no fuel, is reliable, renewable and doesn't pollute.

Against:
Tidal power machines are expensive to build and only provide power for around 10 hours each day, when the tide is actually moving in or out. Not an efficient way of producing electricity.

Glossary and Resources

Arctic Circle An imaginary line that marks the boundary of the frozen region around the North Pole.

atmosphere The thick blanket of air that surrounds the Earth.

bit The sharp tool on the end of a drill that cuts through the rock.

condense To change from a gas to a liquid.

crude oil Oil that is found naturally underground.

derrick The steel frame that holds the drilling equipment at a well.

diesel Fuel similar to petrol that is often used in larger vehicles such as trucks.

drill string A set of linked steel pipes that are attached to a drill bit.

extract To take something out.

fossil fuel A fuel such as coal, oil or gas that is formed underground from the remains of prehistoric plants and animals.

fractionating tower The tall tower in which crude oil is separated or distilled into different liquids and gases.

fuel cell A device that combines hydrogen and oxygen to create electricity that can be used to power a car or building.

generator A machine that turns mechanical energy into electrical energy.

geologist A scientist who studies the Earth.

global warming A warming of the Earth's surface. Many scientists predict that global warming may lead to more floods, droughts and rising sea levels.

greenhouse effect The global warming caused by human-made gases, such as carbon dioxide and methane, that trap the heat from the Sun in the atmosphere.

megawatt (MW) A million watts (a watt is a unit of power). A gigawatt is 1,000 MW.

offshore At sea, not far from the coast.

oil field A region with large reserves of oil ready to be extracted.

oil rig A platform used to drill for oil offshore.

petrol The fuel used in cars; also known as gasoline or gas.

petroleum Crude oil.

plankton Microscopic plants and animals that float in the seas.

production platform A platform that pumps oil from below the seabed.

refinery A plant where crude oil is processed and separated into different liquids and gases.

renewable Something that can be used over and over without running out.

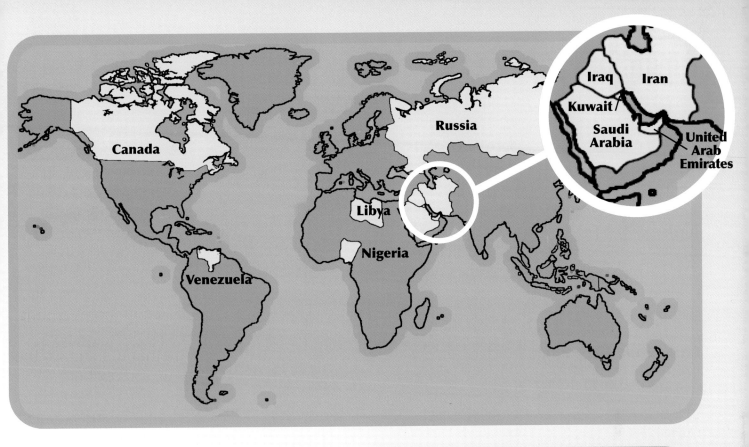

Useful Websites

If you're interested in finding out more about oil, the following websites are helpful:

www.eia.doe.gov/kids/energyfacts

www.energyhog.org/childrens.htm

www.mms.gov/alaska/kids

www.energystar.gov/kids

www.sjgs.com/history.html

www.energyquest.ca.gov/story/chapter08.html

ENERGY FACTS:

Map of Major Oil Nations

In 2009, the ten countries with the largest oil reserves (stores) were:

1 **Saudi Arabia** – 262 billion barrels
2 **Canada** – 179 billion barrels
3 **Iran** – 126 billion barrels
4 **Iraq** – 115 billion barrels
5 **Kuwait** – 101.5 billion barrels
6 **United Arab Emirates** – 97 billion barrels
7 **Venezuela** – 80 billion barrels
8 **Russia** – 60 billion barrels
9 **Libya** – 41 billion barrels
10 **Nigeria** – 36 billion barrels

Further reading

World Issues: Energy Crisis by Ewan McLeish (Aladdin/Watts)

Issues in Our World: Energy Crisis by Ewan McLeish (Aladdin/Watts)

Your Environment: Future Energy by Sally Morgan (Aladdin/Watts)

Saving Our World: New Energy Sources by Nigel Hawkes (Aladdin/Watts)

Our World: Oil by Kate Bedford (Aladdin/Watts)

Resources: Oils and the Environment by Ian Mercer (Franklin Watts)

Environmental Disasters: Oil Spills by Jane Walker (Franklin Watts)

Index

Photocredits

(Abbreviations: t – top, m – middle, b – bottom, l – left, r – right).

All photos istockphoto.com except: 3b, 18ml: courtesy AMEC. 10tl: Comstock. 11mr, 26ml: courtesy BP. 13tr: NASA. 16tl: Photodisc. 16bl: Stockbyte. 26t: courtesy Schilling Robotics, LLC. 26mr: courtesy Morris Architects, Houston, USA. 26bl: Zero Motorcycles, Inc. 27br: USGS.